Symbols of America

U.S. FLAG

TABLE OF CONTENTS

U.S. Flag 3

Glossary 22

Index 24

A Crabtree Seedlings Book

School-to-Home Support for Caregivers and Teachers

This book helps children grow by letting them practice reading. Here are a few guiding questions to help the reader with building his or her comprehension skills. Possible answers appear here in red.

Before Reading:
- What do I think this book is about?
  - *I think this book is about the United States flag.*
  - *I think this book is about the history of the flag.*
- What do I want to learn about this topic?
  - *I want to learn more about how the flag was designed.*
  - *I want to learn more about the stars on the U.S. flag.*

During Reading:
- I wonder why...
  - *I wonder why there are red and white stripes on the U.S. flag.*
  - *I wonder why we have a Flag Day.*
- What have I learned so far?
  - *I have learned that the first flag was sewn by Betsy Ross.*
  - *I have learned that the first flag had 13 stars in a circle.*

After Reading:
- What details did I learn about this topic?
  - *I have learned that the 13 stripes on the flag are for the 13 colonies.*
  - *I have learned that there have been 27 versions of the flag.*
- Read the book again and look for the vocabulary words.
  - *I see the word **symbol** on page 3, and the word **colonies** on page 8. The other glossary words are on pages 22 and 23.*

U.S. FLAG

The United States **flag** is a **symbol** of America.

It has 50 white stars.

The stars are for each **state**.

The flag has 7 red stripes and 6 white stripes.

The 13 stripes are for the 13 **colonies**.

The colonies became the first states.

The Stars and Stripes was the first flag. It had 13 stars in a circle.

Grand Union Flag

There have been 27 versions of the flag.

This flag was made **official** on June 14, 1777.

This day is now known as Flag Day.

It has long been believed that Betsy Ross designed and sewed the first American flag.

In 1958, a 17-year-old high school student named Robert G. Heft designed the current flag for a contest.

In 1814, Francis Scott Key saw the flag after a battle.

He wrote the words to "The Star-Spangled Banner."

The flag has been to many places.

There is a flag on the Moon.

Five American flags have been to the Moon.

Many people have flags at their homes.

They show their **pride** of their country.

Glossary

colonies (kaa-LUH-neez): A group of people from one country living in a new country

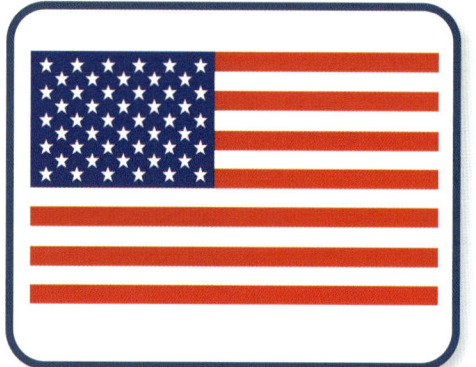

flag (flag): Typically a square cloth that symbolizes a nation

official (uh-FI-shl): Relating to a decision by those in charge

pride (pride): Having respect for something

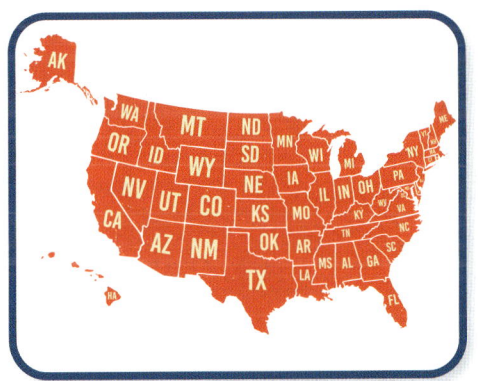

state (stayt): A territory that has a government that is owned by a bigger government

symbol (SIM-bl): A thing that represents something else

Index

America 3, 21
colonies 8, 9
Flag Day 12
Heft, Robert G. 14
Key, Francis Scott 16
Moon 18
Ross, Betsy 14

Written by: Christina Earley
Designed by: Kathy Walsh
Proofreader: Petrice Custance

About the Author

Christina Earley lives in sunny South Florida with her husband and son. She enjoys traveling around the United States and learning about different historical places. Her hobbies include hiking, yoga, and baking.

Photographs: Shutterstock: cover: © kropic1, ©MT511, ©dz; Title Pg: ©MT511, ©dz; Pg 4-21 ©MT511; Pg 3, 23: ©Nathan Bai; Pg 4: © Shabtay; Pg 5 & 23: ©monkographic; Pg 7: © Shabtay; Pg 9, 22: @Wiki; Pg 10: ©Bruce Stanfield; Pg 11: Hoshie @Wiki; Pg 13, 22: ©Kmannn; Pg 15: @Wiki; Pg 16: ©Everett Collection; Pg 17: Library of Congress, Music Division; Pg 19: @NASA; Pg 20: ©WorldStock; Pg 21, 23: ©wavebreakmedia; Pg 22: © charnsitr

Library and Archives Canada Cataloguing in Publication
CIP available at Library and Archives Canada

Library of Congress Cataloging-in-Publication Data
CIP available at Library of Congress

Crabtree Publishing Company
www.crabtreebooks.com   1-800-387-7650

Printed in the U.S.A./072022/CG20220201

Copyright © 2023 **CRABTREE PUBLISHING COMPANY**

All rights reserved. No part of this publication may be reproduced, stored in a retrieval system or be transmitted in any form or by any means, electronic, mechanical, photocopying, recording, or otherwise, without the prior written permission of Crabtree Publishing Company.

Published in the United States
Crabtree Publishing
347 Fifth Avenue, Suite 1402-145
New York, NY, 10016

Published in Canada
Crabtree Publishing
616 Welland Ave.
St. Catharines, Ontario L2M 5V6